The British Museum

THE
LEGEND
OF
TROY

Goldie Hawk • Esther Aarts

This publication accompanies the BP exhibition
Troy: myth and reality at the British Museum
from 21 November 2019 to 8 March 2020.

First published 2019 by Nosy Crow Ltd
The Crow's Nest, 14 Baden Place
Crosby Row, London SE1 1YW
www.nosycrow.com

ISBN 978 1 78800 542 5 (HB)
ISBN 978 1 78800 514 2 (PB)

Nosy Crow and associated logos are trademarks
and/or registered trademarks of Nosy Crow Ltd.

Published in collaboration with the British Museum.

Text © Goldie Hawk 2019
Illustrations © Esther Aarts 2019

The right of Goldie Hawk to be identified as the author
and Esther Aarts to be identified as the illustrator of this work has been asserted.

All photos, unless otherwise stated, are © The Trustees of the British Museum.

A CIP catalogue record for this book is available from the British Library.

Printed in China.
Papers used by Nosy Crow are made from wood
grown in sustainable forests.

1 3 5 7 9 8 6 4 2 (HB)
1 3 5 7 9 8 6 4 2 (PB)

THE
LEGEND
OF
TROY

Goldie Hawk • Esther Aarts

CONTENTS

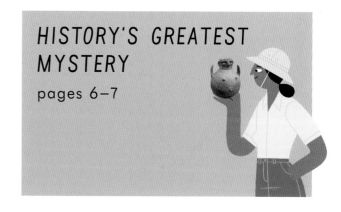

HISTORY'S GREATEST MYSTERY
pages 6–7

WELCOME TO ANCIENT GREECE
pages 8–9

LOVE AND WAR
pages 10–11

THE SIEGE OF TROY
pages 12–13

THE FALL OF TROY
pages 14–15

AN EPIC JOURNEY
pages 16–17

RETURN TO GREECE
pages 18–19

FINDING TROY
pages 20–21

THE TRUTH ABOUT TROY
pages 22–23

TELLING STORIES
pages 24–25

PAINTING PICTURES
pages 26–27

THE LEGEND OF TROY
pages 28–29

INDEX AND
ACKNOWLEDGEMENTS
pages 30–32

HISTORY'S GREATEST MYSTERY

THE STORY OF THE DESTRUCTION OF THE ANCIENT CITY OF TROY IS ONE OF THE WORLD'S GREATEST TALES.

It has been told in books, plays, poems, art and music for almost 3,000 years. And it is still being told today.

It is a story of adventure, war, love and death, with many twists and turns and thousands of characters – from fearsome warriors and powerful goddesses to six-headed sea monsters and a man-eating giant.

One hundred and fifty years ago, the legend of Troy was thought to be entirely made up. But more recently, archaeologists and scholars believe that they have found the ancient city.

But will we ever find out the truth about what really happened to Troy?

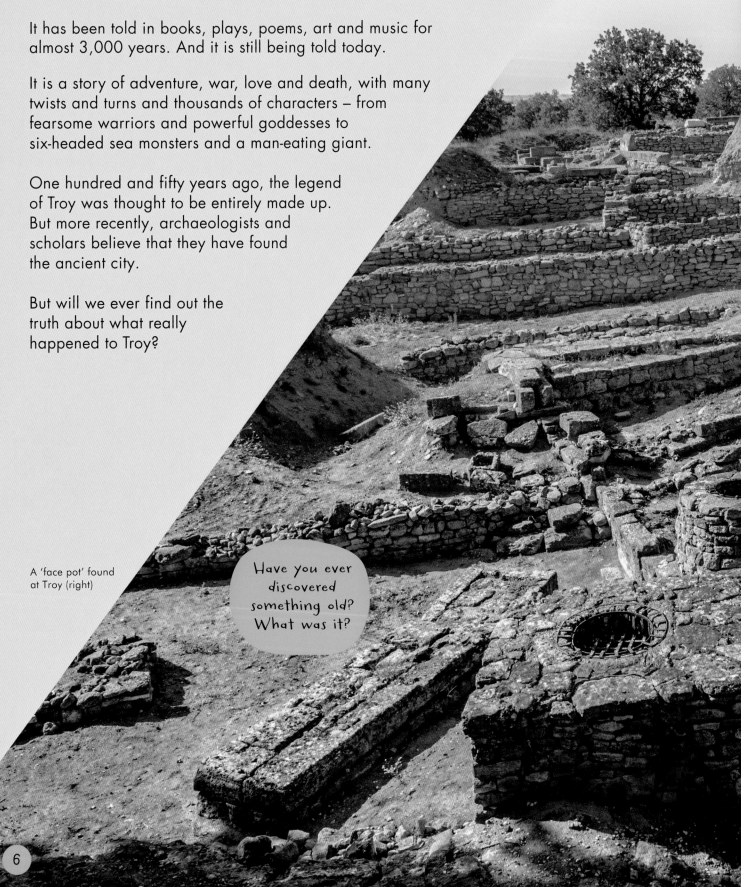

A 'face pot' found at Troy (right)

Have you ever discovered something old? What was it?

TOP TIP

'BC' stands for 'Before Christ'. If you see 'BC' after a date, this means it is the number of years before Christians believe Jesus Christ was born (about 2,000 years ago).

So, if an object was made in 500 BC, it is around 2,500 years old.

KEY WORDS

A **LEGEND** is a story that many people believe to be true, even though there may not be any proof that it really happened.

An **ARCHAEOLOGIST** is a person who finds and studies objects from past and present civilisations.

A **SCHOLAR** is a person who specialises in studying a particular subject.

7

WELCOME TO ANCIENT GREECE

THE ANCIENT GREEKS WERE VERY CLEVER. THEY CAME UP WITH INCREDIBLY IMPORTANT IDEAS, BUILT AMAZING BUILDINGS AND HAD THEIR OWN SPECIAL ALPHABET.

Thousands of years ago, life in ancient Greece was very different to life in Greece now. Ancient Greece did not even cover quite the same area as the modern country.

WE GREEKS LIVE IN CITY-STATES. EACH CITY IS ALMOST LIKE ITS OWN COUNTRY.

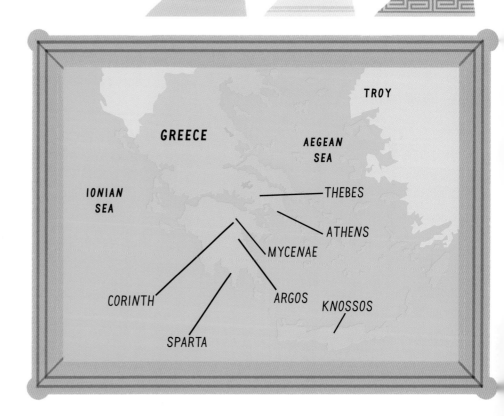

Religion was very important. The ancient Greeks believed in many gods and built elaborate temples for them, with beautiful statues inside. The gods and goddesses were a bit like humans, but a lot more powerful. They watched over the ancient Greeks from their home on Mount Olympus, interfering with their lives and arguing with each other.

I'M HERMES, THE MESSENGER GOD!

THE PEOPLE OF ATHENS CARVED US ON A BIG TEMPLE!

A scene carved into a Greek temple called the Parthenon

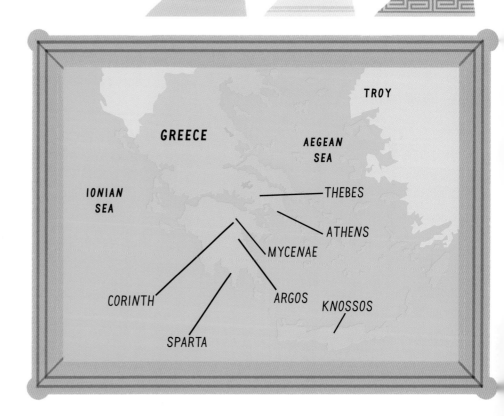

GODS AND GODDESSES

Here are some of the most important Greek gods and goddesses.

WATCH ME THROW THIS THING!

I'VE BEEN TO MORE MARRIAGES THAN ANYONE HERE!

I BET YOU'RE NOT AS WISE AS ME!

WATCH OUT FOR MY TRIDENT!

I'M MIGHTY APHRODITE!

ZEUS
King of the gods and god of the sky.

HERA
Wife (and sister!) of Zeus, and goddess of women, marriage and family.

ATHENA
Daughter of Zeus, and goddess of wisdom and war.

POSEIDON
Brother of Zeus and Hera, and god of the sea.

APHRODITE
Goddess of love and beauty, and a bit of a trouble-maker.

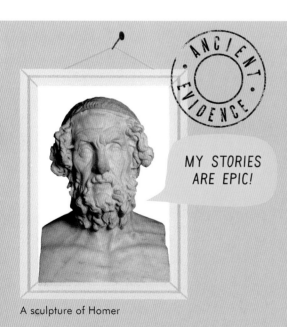

ANCIENT EVIDENCE

MY STORIES ARE EPIC!

A sculpture of Homer

TELLING STORIES

The ancient Greeks were brilliant storytellers. They told many stories about their gods, goddesses and fellow Greeks, which they used to explain their world and to spread important messages and lessons about life.

The Trojan Cycle is a collection of ancient Greek epic poems, telling the story of Troy. Two of the most famous are the *Iliad* and the *Odyssey*. The Greeks belived a poet called Homer composed them. He probably lived in the 8th or 7th century BC.

KEY WORDS

A **CITY-STATE** is a city and country in one.

MOUNT OLYMPUS is the mountain home of the ancient Greek gods.

HOMER was a famous poet in ancient Greece. People believed he was blind.

EPIC means something that is both very long and that tells the story of a heroic or legendary figure from a country's past.

LOVE AND WAR

THE TROJANS AND THE GREEKS HAD BEEN RIVALS FOR YEARS, BUT THE TROJAN WAR BEGAN BECAUSE TWO PEOPLE FELL IN LOVE: PARIS AND HELEN.

Paris was a Trojan, and the son of King Priam and Queen Hecuba of Troy. When he was born, it was predicted that he would cause the fall of Troy. So the king and queen left their baby on a hill, hoping he would die. But Paris survived and was raised by a shepherd instead.

A DANGEROUS DECISION

Years later, Paris was guarding his sheep when Hermes, messenger of the Greek gods, arrived with three goddesses: Hera, Athena and Aphrodite. They had come from a wedding where there had been an argument over a golden apple, which was to be given to the most beautiful goddess. Zeus, king of the gods, didn't want to choose, so he sent Hermes to ask Paris to make the decision.

Each goddess begged Paris to choose her.

A pot decorated wi[th] the golden apple scen[e]

PICK ME AND YOU SHALL HAVE THE LOVE OF THE MOST BEAUTIFUL WOMAN IN THE WORLD!

APHRODITE

PICK ME AND YOU WILL WIN ANY WAR!

PICK ME AND YOU WILL BE RICH AND POWERFUL!

HERA

ATHENA

Paris picked Aphrodite, who explained that the most beautiful woman was called Helen and lived in Sparta in Greece.

What she didn't tell him was that Helen was married to Menelaus, the king of Sparta.

KING MENELAUS

HELEN

Part of a plaque showing Helen and her attendants

THE PRINCE RETURNS

Not long afterwards, Paris took part in the Trojan games. When he defeated all of the other princes, they realised that he must be their brother. King Priam felt so guilty for abandoning his son as a baby that he decided it was worth risking the fall of Troy to have Paris back.

Soon after, Paris was sent with some other Trojans to Sparta, in Greece. As soon as Paris met Helen, they fell in love, just as Aphrodite had promised, and Helen agreed to run away with Paris to Troy.

A pot showing Paris arriving to take Helen to Troy

11

THE SIEGE OF TROY

KING MENELAUS WAS FURIOUS WHEN HELEN LEFT, AND ASKED HIS BROTHER, AGAMEMNON, AND MANY OTHER GREEKS, TO BRING HER BACK. THEY GATHERED AN ARMY AND SET SAIL FOR TROY.

When they arrived, they could not break down Troy's strong walls, but they refused to leave without Helen. King Priam, Paris's father, gathered his own army to protect Troy. Ten years of fighting began, with many people dying on both sides.

To make things even more difficult, the Greek gods started meddling with the war too, picking and switching sides.

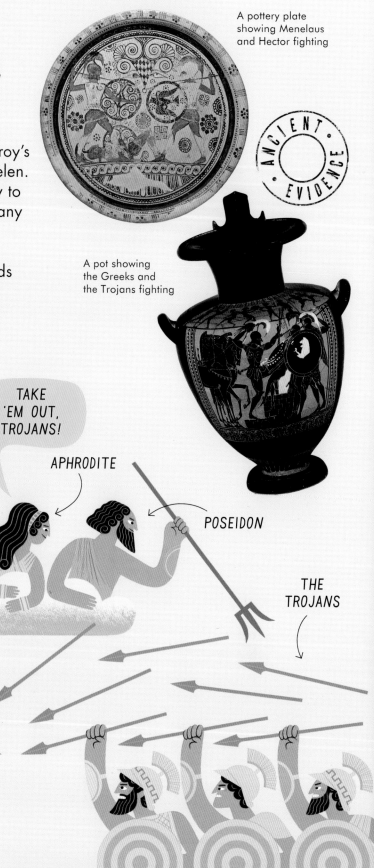

A pottery plate showing Menelaus and Hector fighting

ANCIENT · EVIDENCE

A pot showing the Greeks and the Trojans fighting

ZEUS

GO ON, GREEKS!

TAKE 'EM OUT, TROJANS!

APHRODITE

POSEIDON

THE GREEKS

THE TROJANS

KEY WORDS

A SIEGE is when a town or city is surrounded by an army in order to cut off supplies of food and water and force the city to surrender.

AGAMEMNON was the brother of King Menelaus and commander of the Greek army.

ACHILLES was one of Greece's best warriors.

IMMORTAL is when something or someone lives forever.

PATROCLUS was Achilles' very best friend and a Greek warrior.

HECTO was Pari brother an great Tro warrior

THE ILIAD

Homer's story, the *Iliad*, begins nine years into the battle. Achilles – the Greeks' best warrior – was refusing to fight after getting into an argument with the Greek king.

The Greeks needed Achilles because he was a brilliant fighter and his body was immortal, except for his heel.

Without Achilles, the Greeks started to lose, so Achilles' best friend, Patroclus, disguised himself in Achilles' armour, hoping the Trojans would see him and run away with fear.

It worked . . . until the god Apollo revealed who Patroclus really was, and he was quickly killed by Hector, who was one of Paris's brothers and a great Trojan warrior.

ANCIENT EVIDENCE

A cup showing Achilles sulkily refusing to fight

DRAMATIC DEATHS

After this, Achilles started fighting again, wearing new armour made by the gods. He killed Hector in a dramatic fight, but soon afterwards, Paris shot Achilles in the heel and he died too.

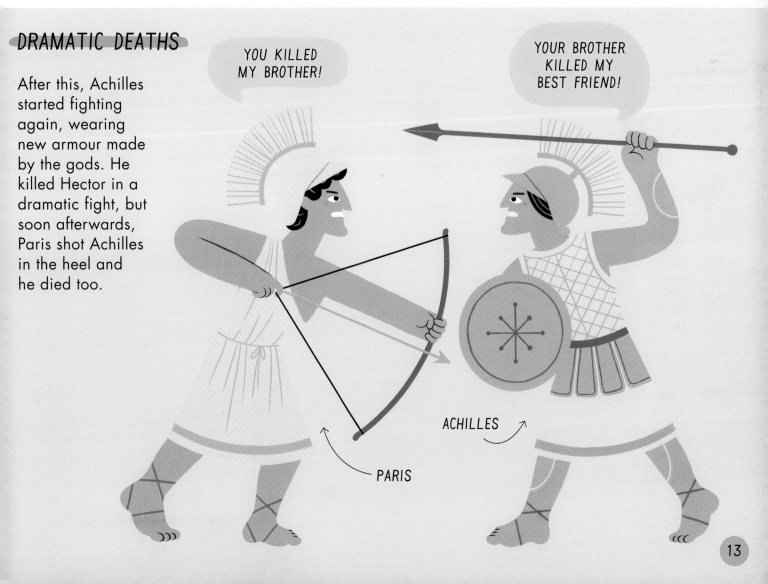

ACHILLES

13

THE FALL OF TROY

MANY MORE TRAGEDIES TOOK PLACE ON BOTH SIDES,
UNTIL THE GREEKS FINALLY MANAGED TO KILL PARIS.
BUT THEY STILL HADN'T MANAGED TO GET HELEN BACK.

After ten years of fighting, everyone was desperate to end
the war. Eventually, the Greek hero Odysseus came up
with a clever plan to beat the Trojans.

A DEADLY GIFT

Odysseus and the Greek army built an enormous wooden
horse, which some of Greece's most talented warriors hid
inside. The rest of the army then left the horse outside the
gates of Troy and pretended to sail back to Greece.

> Greek soldiers hid inside
> the Trojan horse. They
> had to keep very quiet!

> TEE HEE!

> LET'S JUST LEAVE
> THIS HUGE HORSE
> HERE AND GO BACK
> TO GREECE!

> SHHH!
> THEY'LL
> HEAR YOU!

The Trojans believed the Greeks had gone and left the horse as an offering to the gods to protect them on their journey. So they took the horse inside the city and spent the whole night celebrating the end of the war.

THE END OF THE WAR

While the Trojans were having fun, the Greek ships sailed silently back to Troy. Once the Trojans were asleep, the Greek soldiers inside the horse crept out and opened the city gates for the rest of their army. The Greeks then destroyed Troy from the inside, took Helen back and finally won the war!

King Menelaus had been planning to punish Helen for causing the war, but when he saw her he decided he still loved her, and she became his wife again.

A fresco showing the Trojan horse being pulled in by the Trojans

KEY WORDS

A
TRAGEDY
is an event that is very sad and distressing.

The
TROJAN HORSE
was a huge wooden horse, built by the Greek army, which Greek warriors hid inside.

An
OFFERING
is a gift given to the gods.

A
FRESCO
is a painting made on a wall while the plaster is still wet.

15

AN EPIC JOURNEY

ONCE THE WAR WAS OVER, THE GREEKS TRAVELLED HOME. BUT ODYSSEUS, KING OF ITHACA AND THE MAN BEHIND THE CLEVER TROJAN HORSE IDEA, HAD THE MOST DIFFICULT JOURNEY OF ALL . . .

THE ODYSSEY

Homer's poem the *Odyssey* is all about Odysseus's terrible journey. First, his fleet of 12 ships were separated from the rest of the Greek army in an enormous storm and washed up in a strange land. His soldiers were offered lotus fruit to eat, which made them forget about everything except eating more fruit. Luckily, Odysseus managed to force them back on to their ships and they sailed away.

MAN-EATING MONSTERS

Next, Odysseus and his soldiers landed at an island ruled by a cruel Cyclops called Polyphemus. He locked the men in a cave with his sheep and started to eat them alive. One night, when Polyphemus was sleeping, Odysseus blinded him with a sharpened pole. Then, when the sheep were let out to graze the next day, the soldiers clung to their bellies.

The Cyclops felt the back of each sheep to make sure none of the men had escaped, but he didn't feel underneath, so the soldiers got away.

THIS IS ITCHY!

HANG IN THERE!

A WASTED GIFT

Odysseus and his soldiers soon arrived at the island of Aeolus, guardian of the winds, who kindly tied the storm winds up in a bag for Odysseus, so he would have an easy journey home.

But the rest of the soldiers thought the bag might contain treasure, and opened it as soon as they set sail. A storm so fierce was released that only Odysseus and one of his ships survived.

UH-OH!

KEY WORDS

LOTUS FRUIT
was a magical fruit that made a person forget about everything but eating more fruit, trapping them forever.

A
CYCLOPS
was a huge, one-eyed giant.

AEOLUS
was a Greek god and the guardian of the winds.

RETURN TO GREECE

ODYSSEUS'S JOURNEY WAS STILL FAR FROM OVER.
SHAKEN AND EXHAUSTED, HE AND HIS REMAINING MEN
ARRIVED AT THE ISLAND HOME OF A WITCH CALLED
CIRCE, WHO TURNED ODYSSEUS'S
SOLDIERS INTO PIGS!

Just in time, Hermes,
the messenger god,
appeared and gave
Odysseus a plant
to protect him from
Circe's spells.

Amazed that her magic
did not work on him, the
witch fell in love with
Odysseus and turned his
soldiers back into men.

ODYSSEUS

CIRCE

ODYSSEUS

YOU WILL
NEVER WIN!

YOU'RE
JUST AN
OLD MAN!

LOST AT SEA

After leaving Circe's island, they had to sail past the Sirens, who could lure men to their deaths with their singing. As if that wasn't bad enough, they also had to sail their ship between two monsters – Scylla, who had six heads, and Charybdis, a whirlpool that sucked ships underwater.

Soon afterwards, Odysseus lost his final ship and all his men to an angry god and was held captive on an island by a nymph called Calypso. After seven years he escaped on a tiny raft with the help of Zeus and Hermes, who felt sorry for him.

SCYLLA

CHARYBDIS

ANCIENT · EVIDENCE

A pot showing Odysseus's ship sailing past the Sirens

THE FINAL FIGHT

Disguised as an old man, Odysseus reached his home at last to find Greek noblemen fighting over his belongings and his wife, Penelope. Odysseus told his son, Telemachus, who he really was, and together they secretly removed all the nobles' weapons from the palace.

Believing Odysseus was dead, Penelope finally agreed to marry whoever could shoot an arrow from Odysseus's bow, but all the noblemen who tried, failed. Still in disguise, Odysseus shot the arrow perfectly. When the nobles realised who he was, they looked for their weapons so they could fight, but Odysseus killed them all. Reunited with his wife and son, Odysseus's journey was finally over.

HE LOOKS RATHER FAMILIAR!

TELEMACHUS

ENELOPE

FINDING TROY

SO WHERE IS TROY? DID IT REALLY EXIST? IN THE PAST, EXPERTS BELIEVED TROY WAS NOTHING MORE THAN A STORY. BUT ABOUT 150 YEARS AGO, A GERMAN BUSINESSMAN CALLED HEINRICH SCHLIEMANN MADE AN AMAZING DISCOVERY . . .

Schliemann was an amateur archaeologist and desperate to prove that Homer's *Iliad* was more than just a story. After meeting an English archaeologist called Frank Calvert, who had done a lot of research, Schliemann decided that Troy was most likely buried under a mound in Hissarlik in northwest Anatolia, now Turkey.

Calvert had already started digging in the area and had found some interesting objects, but he didn't have enough money to do a full excavation.

Schliemann had a lot of money. So, starting in 1870, he dug down as deep as he could and discovered a buried city, which he claimed was the real Troy.

In this city, he found gold jewellery, vessels of gold and silver, a copper shield, seven copper daggers, 14 copper axes, and much more. He named them 'Priam's Treasure', after King Priam of Troy in the *Iliad*.

SCHLIEMANN

CALVERT

ANCIENT · EVIDENCE

A watercolour painting of Schliemann's excavation

FACT OR FICTION?

After Schliemann told the world about his discovery, people got very excited. But many experts questioned Schliemann's findings, since he wasn't properly trained.

Schliemann also got in a lot of trouble for smuggling the treasure out of Troy and even giving the precious jewellery to his wife, Sophia, to wear. At the end of the Second World War, the treasures were taken to Russia, where they still remain today.

ANCIENT EVIDENCE

A photograph of `Priam's Treasure´

Have you ever found anything buried in the ground?

SOPHIA

SCHLIEMANN

Three silver vessels found by Schliemann

KEY WORDS

A **MOUND** is a man-made hill or mountain, sometimes created when buildings are buried under other materials.

HISSARLIK is a place in northwest Anatolia, Turkey.

An **EXCAVATION** is an organised archaeological dig.

A **VESSEL** is a container used to hold liquid.

21

THE TRUTH ABOUT TROY

TODAY, MOST ARCHAEOLOGISTS BELIEVE THAT SCHLIEMANN WAS
BOTH RIGHT AND WRONG ABOUT HAVING FOUND THE CITY OF TROY.
BUT HOW CAN SOMEONE BE RIGHT AND WRONG AT THE SAME TIME?

Today we know that the mound of Hissarlik concealed not just one ruined city, but
at least nine cities, all built on top of each other in layers over time. The city on the
top belongs to the Roman period, then comes the Greek city, and under that seven
cities from the Bronze Age. 'Priam's Treasure' comes from the second city from the
bottom, and so belongs to the Early Bronze Age.

A glass bo

A cup with two
large handles

A 'face pot'

A decorated
dish

A bottle

A cup with two
large handles

A silver
coin

A stone mosaic

A cup with
one
handle

A bowl

A vessel in the
shape of a pig

What do you
think these
objects were
used for?

DESTROYED EVIDENCE

Experts believe that the sixth or seventh layer might be the setting which inspired Homer's stories. It is dated to the Late Bronze Age, when there was contact between Greeks and Trojans. The sixth layer was clearly a very important city that was destroyed by an earthquake. The seventh layer was less impressive, but some archaeologists see evidence for a siege, which they connect with the Trojan War.

Archaeologists nowadays dig very carefully, but Schliemann was a pioneer and wasn't trained. At that time, nobody knew how to recognise the Bronze Age, so he just dug a trench straight down, as deep as he could. This means he probably dug right through the city Homer talked about without realising.

Schliemann's excavations destroyed most of the evidence of the other cities in the mound of Hissarlik, but archaeologists now know that some of the cities extended across the surrounding area, so there is still a lot left to discover.

KEY

- 9th layer (85 BC–700 AD)
- 8th layer (900–85 BC)
- 7th layer (1300–900 BC)
- 6th layer (1750–1300 BC)
- 5th layer (2000–1750 BC)
- 4th layer (2200–2000 BC)
- 3rd layer (2300–2200 BC)
- 2nd layer (2550–2300 BC)
- 1st layer (3000–2550 BC)

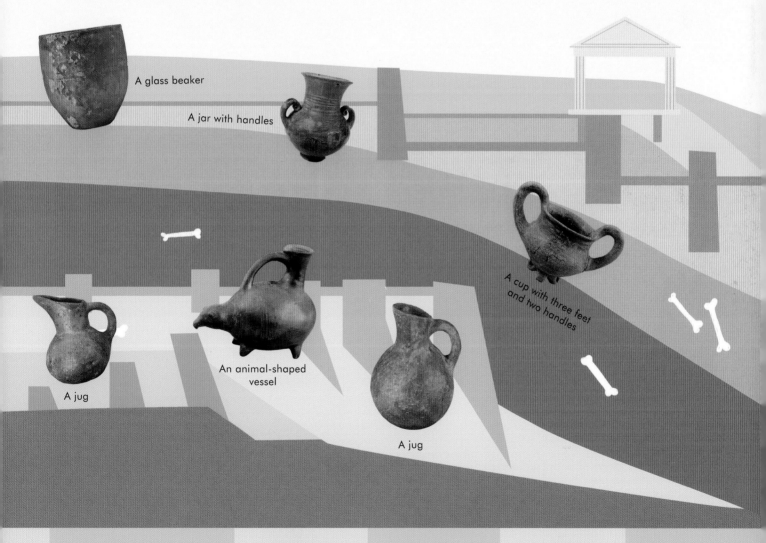

A glass beaker

A jar with handles

A cup with three feet and two handles

A jug

An animal-shaped vessel

A jug

KEY WORDS

The **BRONZE AGE** began in around 3000 BC and ended in around 1000 BC. It is divided into Early, Middle and Late.

A **MOSAIC** is created by arranging together small pieces of coloured tile, stone or glass.

A **PIONEER** is someone who develops new ideas or techniques.

A **TRENCH** is part of an excavation and has straight edges.

EVIDENCE is physical proof of something.

TELLING STORIES

IMAGINE TRYING TO MEMORISE 28,000 LINES OF POETRY. IT MIGHT SEEM IMPOSSIBLE, BUT THAT'S WHAT THE ANCIENT GREEK POET HOMER DID!

... AND THEN HE WAS KILLED WITH AN ARROW!

HOMER

WOW!

NO WAY!

The epic tales about the Trojan War were originally designed to be recited and listened to, not written down and read. People liked them so much that in time they wrote them down. Now they have been translated into many different languages.

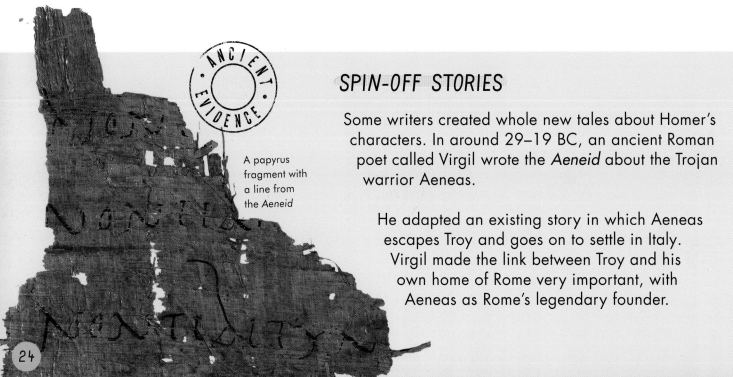

ANCIENT · EVIDENCE

A papyrus fragment with a line from the *Aeneid*

SPIN-OFF STORIES

Some writers created whole new tales about Homer's characters. In around 29–19 BC, an ancient Roman poet called Virgil wrote the *Aeneid* about the Trojan warrior Aeneas.

He adapted an existing story in which Aeneas escapes Troy and goes on to settle in Italy. Virgil made the link between Troy and his own home of Rome very important, with Aeneas as Rome's legendary founder.

LOVE STORIES

In the medieval period, some of the stories about Troy became love stories. One of the most famous was Geoffrey Chaucer's *Troilus and Criseyde,* written in the 1380s. In Chaucer's story, a Trojan warrior called Troilus falls in love with a Trojan woman called Criseyde.

But Criseyde's father, who has joined the Greek army, arranges for Criseyde to join him on the Greek side. Criseyde promises Troilus she will return, but instead falls in love with Diomedes, a Greek warrior, while Troilus dies in battle.

CRISEYDE

ERR...YES, OF COURSE!

How would you rewrite Homer's stories?

YOU WILL COME BACK, WON'T YOU?

DIOMEDES

TROILUS

MODERN STORIES

Modern writers also rewrite Homer's stories. Some have written books or poems that focus on the women in the *Iliad* and the *Odyssey,* some have moved the location of the stories to Africa and the Caribbean, and some have compared Odysseus's long journey to the migrations many people have to take across the world, away from their homes.

Romare Bearden's screenprint, *The Sirens' Song*

PAINTING PICTURES

THE STORY OF TROY HAS BEEN FOUND IN ART THROUGHOUT HISTORY:

painted on walls, canvases and pottery; carved on to pins and sculptures; and even woven into tapestries and clothing. Each piece of artwork tells us more about why the story has fascinated people for so long.

Do you have any clothes that tell a story?

THANKS, IT'S VINTAGE!

WHAT A LOVELY TROJAN HORSE YOU HAVE ON YOUR DRESS!

Many artists have painted or sculpted Helen of Troy, the beautiful woman whose love affair with Paris started the Trojan War. Some artists imagined she would feel guilty about causing the war and the burning of Troy, while others have painted her looking strong and confident, like a Greek goddess.

A painting of Helen by Edward Burne-Jones

A sculpture of Helen by Antonio Canova

A painting of Helen by Evelyn de Morgan

WAR IN ART

Achilles and Hector, two of the most famous Greek and Trojan warriors, have also been painted and sculpted by many artists, especially during wartime. Some artists made the battles look exciting and heroic, while others made them look very scary and sad.

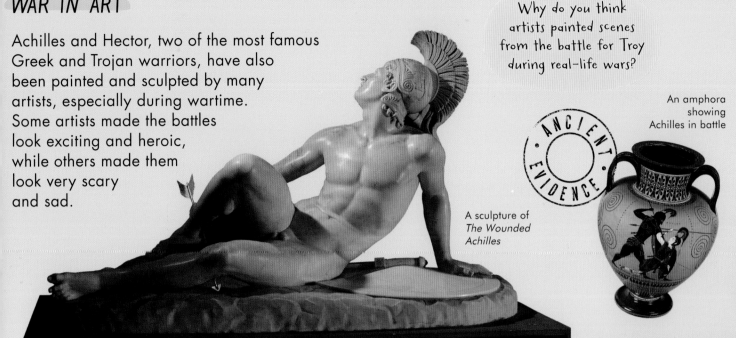

Why do you think artists painted scenes from the battle for Troy during real-life wars?

ANCIENT · EVIDENCE

An amphora showing Achilles in battle

A sculpture of *The Wounded Achilles*

A NEVER-ENDING STORY

An artist called John Flaxman designed a silver gilt shield, which he called *The Shield of Achilles*, in 1821. It recreates a shield described by Homer in the *Iliad*. Some art historians have suggested that Flaxman used the shape of the shield to show how the story of the *Iliad* is never-ending: it keeps going through history, like a circle or a wheel turning.

The Shield of Achilles, designed by John Flaxman and made by Philip Rundell

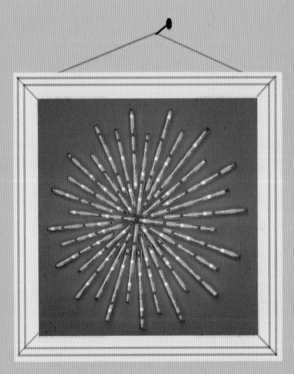

Spencer Finch's installation, *The Shield of Achilles*

DAWN OVER TROY

More recently, in 2013, an American artist called Spencer Finch created an art installation called *The Shield of Achilles* made from fluorescent lights. Finch said he was inspired to make it because light is one of the things that hasn't changed since the battle of Troy.

KEY WORDS

In an
ART INSTALLATION
art is used to create an environment that each viewer experiences in their own way.

An
AMPHORA
is a tall jug used to store wine and oil.

THE LEGEND OF TROY

SO, WHY ARE WE STILL INTERESTED IN THE LEGEND OF TROY, EVEN THOUGH WE MIGHT NEVER FIND OUT THE TRUTH ABOUT WHAT REALLY HAPPENED?

Perhaps it's because although the world has changed hugely over the past three thousand years, the things people care about haven't changed much at all. We might live in a world of computers, smartphones and driverless cars, but people still argue, fall in love and go to war, just as they did in the *Iliad* and the *Odyssey*.

Or perhaps it's because we're still trying to work out who was right and who was wrong in the story of Troy, just like everyone who has ever read or heard the story.

A vessel in the shape of a bull's head

A plaque showing the judgement of Paris

A pot decorated with a painting of an octopus

A wine-bowl showing the wedding where the goddesses argued

A jar with a striped design

We will probably never know whether the Troy in Homer's *Iliad* and *Odyssey* really existed, but one thing we do know is that the story of this legendary city has fascinated people for thousands of years.

And through retelling the story of Troy, we are able to travel back in time to a world that was very different from – but not completely unlike – our own.

A fresco showing Odysseus and the Sirens

A pot showing Achilles fighting Hector

A pot showing Achilles and Ajax playing a game

A 'face pot'

DO YOU THINK THESE CHARACTERS WERE RIGHT OR WRONG TO BEHAVE THE WAY THEY DID?

KING PRIAM

King Priam left his baby son to die on a hillside because he believed this was necessary to save his city.

HELEN

Helen left her husband, Menelaus, to run away to Troy with Paris, but she had never wanted to marry Menelaus in the first place – she had been forced to.

ODYSSEUS

Odysseus was a liar and a killer, but he was also clever and brave and all he wanted to do was get home to his wife and family.

Why do you think the legend of Troy has interested people for so long?

INDEX

All objects, unless otherwise stated, are from the collection of the British Museum.

Page 6–7:

A photograph of 'the ruins of Troy' in Canakkale, Turkey ©Shutterstock/epic_images

A 'face pot' found at Troy Troy, Turkey, 2500–1800 BC Staatliche Museen zu Berlin, Museum für Vor- und Frühgeschichte, photo: Claudia Plamp

Pages 8–9:

A scene carved into a Greek temple called the Parthenon Athens, Greece, 438–432 BC

A sculpture of Homer Baiae, Italy, 2nd century AD

Pages 10–11:

A pot decorated with the golden apple scene Found in Capua, Italy; from Attica, Greece, c. 470 BC

Part of a plaque showing Helen and her attendants Found in La Banditaccia, Italy; from Etruria, Italy, 560–550 BC

Pages 12–13:

A pot showing Paris arriving to take Helen to Troy Campania, Italy, c. 350–320 BC

A plate showing Menelaus and Hector fighting Found in Kamiros, Greece; from Kos, Greece, c. 600 BC

A pot showing the Greeks and the Trojans fighting Found in Vulci, Italy; from Attica, Greece, c. 520 BC

A cup showing Achilles sulkily refusing to fight Found in Vulci, Italy; from Attica, Greece, c. 470 BC

Page 15:

A fresco showing the Trojan horse being pulled in to Troy by the Trojans, Pompeii, Italy, 1st century AD, Reproduced by permission of the Ministero dei Beni e delle Attività Culturali e del Turismo – National Archaeological Museum Naples

Page 19:

A pot showing Odysseus' ship sailing past the Sirens Found in Vulci, Italy; from Attica, Greece, c. 480–470 BC

Page 20–21:

A watercolour painting of Schliemann's excavation William Simpson, 1877

A photograph of 'Priam's Treasure' From the Atlas Trojanischer Alterthumer, 1874

Three silver vessels found by Schliemann Troy, Turkey, c. 2300 BC, Staatliche Museen zu Berlin, Museum für Vor- und Frühgeschichte, photo: Claudia Plamp

Pages 22–23:

A stone mosaic Troy, Turkey, 4th century AD

A bottle Troy, Turkey, 85 BC–700 AD

A silver coin
Troy, Turkey,
900–85 BC

cup with two large handles
oy, Turkey, 1300–1100 BC, Staatliche Museen
Berlin, Museum für Vor- und Frühgeschichte,
oto: Klaus Göken

A jar with handles
Troy, Turkey,
1900–1700 BC
Staatliche Museen
zu Berlin, Museum
für Vor- und
Frühgeschichte,
photo: Claudia Plamp

A glass beaker
Troy, Turkey,
85 BC–700 AD

*A cup with two
large handles*
Troy, Turkey,
c. 1200 BC

cup with one handle
oy, Turkey, 1300–900 BC, Staatliche
useen zu Berlin, Museum für Vor- und
ühgeschichte, photo: Claudia Plamp

essel in the shape of a pig
oy, Turkey, 1800–1100 BC, Staatliche
useen zu Berlin, Museum für Vor- und
hgeschichte, photo: Jürgen Liepe

A bowl
Troy, Turkey,
3000–2550 BC
Staatliche Museen zu
Berlin, Museum für
Vor- und Frühgeschichte,
photo: Claudia Plamp

A glass bottle
Troy, Turkey,
85 BC–700 AD

A cup with three feet and two handles
Troy, Turkey, 2050–1900 BC, Staatliche Museen
zu Berlin, Museum für Vor- und Frühgeschichte,
photo: Klaus Göken

An animal-shaped vessel
Troy, Turkey,
2600–1800 BC
Staatliche Museen zu
Berlin, Museum für
Vor- und Frühgeschichte,
photo: Claudia Plamp

A jug
Troy, Turkey,
2550–2200 BC
Staatliche Museen zu Berlin,
Museum für Vor- und
Frühgeschichte,
photo: Claudia Plamp

A jug
Troy, Turkey,
3000–2550 BC
Staatliche Museen zu
Berlin, Museum für
Vor- und Frühgeschichte,
photo: Claudia Plamp

A decorated dish
Troy, Turkey,
900–85 BC

Page 24–25:

*A papyrus fragment with a line
from the Aeneid*
Hawara, Egypt, 1st century AD,
on loan from University College
London, Institute of Archaeology

*Romare Bearden's screenprint,
The Sirens' Song*
1979, purchased as the Gift of Richard A.
Simms, National Gallery of Art, Washington
2013.142.3 © Romare Bearden Foundation/
VAGA at ARS, NY and DACS, London 2019

Page 26–27:

*A painting of Helen
(Helen's Tears)*
Edward Burne-Jones,
1882–98

A sculpture of Helen
Antonio Canova
After 1812
© Victoria and Albert
Museum, London

*A painting
of Helen*
Evelyn de
Morgan
1898,
De Morgan
Collection,
courtesy of the
© De Morgan
Foundation
/ Bridgeman
Images

A sculpture of The Wounded Achilles
Filippo Albacini, 1825 © The Devonshire Collections, Chatsworth. Reproduced by permission of Chatsworth Settlement Trustees

An amphora showing Achilles in battle
Found in Vulci, Italy; from Attica, Greece, c. 530–525 BC

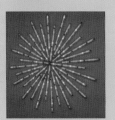

The Shield of Achilles
Spencer Finch 2013, image courtesy the artist

The Shield of Achilles
designed by John Flaxman, 1821, made by Philip Rundell, 1822
© National Trust Images/John Hammond

Page 28–29:

A vessel in the shape of a bull's head
Karpathos, Greece, c. 1425–1300 BC

A plaque showing the judgement of Paris
Found in La Banditaccia, Italy; from Etruria, Italy, 560–550 BC

A wine-bowl showing the wedding where the goddesses argued
Attica, Greece, c. 580–570 BC

A pot decorated with a painting of an octopus
Ialysus, Greece, c. 1390–1325 BC

A jar with a striped design
Ialysus, Greece, c. 1375–1300 BC

A fresco showing Odysseus and the Sirens
Pompeii, Italy, 1st century AD

A pot showing Achilles fighting Hector
Found in Caere, Italy; from Attica, Greece, c. 490–460 BC

A pot showing Achilles and Ajax playing a game
Found in Chiusi, Italy; from Attica, Greece, c. 530 BC

A 'face pot'
Troy, Turkey, c. 2500–2000 BC

ACKNOWLEDGEMENTS

With special thanks to the team at the British Museum:
Victoria Donnellan, Alexandra Villing, Lesley Fitton, Kathleen Bloomfield, Claudia Bloch and Bethany Holmes.

PUBLISHER'S NOTE

This book was created for children, to educate but even more importantly to entertain. Although every attempt at factual accuracy has been made, it is not within the scope of this book to present an exhaustive, academic treatment of this fascinating subject. Any errors, omissions or misinterpretations are ours, not those of the British Museum or its experts.

USE THESE STICKERS ON YOUR
ODYSSEY STICKER SCENE!

I FEEL
SICK!